Acceptance and Commitment Skills

for Medicine

Dr James Fullick

First published by FullScript Ltd, 2023

Copyright © James Fullick, 2023

All rights reserved.

No portion of this book may be reproduced in any form or by any electronic, mechanical or other means, now known or hereafter invented, including photocopying and recording, or in any information storage or retrieval system, without written permission from the publisher or author.

Important note

This book is not intended as a substitute for medical advice or treatment. Any person with a condition requiring medical attention should consult a qualified medical practitioner or suitable therapist.

This publication is designed to provide accurate and authoritative information in regard to the subject matter covered. It is sold with the understanding that neither the author nor the publisher is engaged in rendering psychological, legal, or other professional services.

A CIP catalogue record for this book
is available from the British Library.

ISBN: 979-8-84950-162-8

FullScript Ltd

To my wife and daughter,

and to too many colleagues lost along the way

Prevention is better than cure. A career in medicine and the myriad of opportunities that are encompassed by this broad term, has the potential to be a great career choice. That said, it can also be a very difficult journey. There are casualties along the way; from those personally affected, to health care systems, and to wider society which can ill afford to lose doctors who have been highly invested in. These people should not be ignored.

For those affected personally, changing careers and deciding to leave medicine can be both an individual and family tragedy; but it can also, in some instances be lifesaving. There will always be right reasons why some people leave a medical career; right, being a positive decision that is both good for them and those around them. However, where there are things that can be done to help prevent someone leaving for the wrong reasons, we should endeavor to embrace those opportunities.

Dr James Fullick, in his book 'Acceptance and Commitment Skills for Medicine', presents us with his own experience and subsequent route out of a disillusioned, disenchanted, and despairing relationship with medicine. He offers us, in an easily readable format, a branch of behavioural psychology as a way to better understand why we may see things the way we do, why that can lead to burnout and unhappiness, and a constructive way to implement changes to our perceptions in order to enable us to make ourselves happier, and our medical careers more sustainable.

Preventing burnout and moral despair is better than trying to pick up the pieces after temporarily stepping away, or completely leaving a medical career. Physical training, by eating healthily, running, cycling or swimming is widely accepted. Looking after our psychological wellbeing with mental health training is now becoming more common place. This book provides a means of training our minds to be kinder to ourselves, to understand our own and others' criticisms, and ultimately to enjoy medicine without it damaging us.

Dr Jack Parry-Jones
MBBS BSc FRCP FFICM
Consultant in Adult Intensive Care Medicine
Cardiff

Modern professional healthcare workplaces are extraordinarily fast-paced and high-pressured environments to work in, so much so, that intense stress and burnout are practically the norm. Acceptance and Commitment Therapy (ACT) is a contemporary behavioural approach, grounded in a solid evidence base, that has been developed to help individuals manage the impact of stress of such environments by building and strengthening effective psychological skills. In this book, Dr James Fullick sets out a manual, designed specifically for medical professionals, that takes you through the cutting-edge psychological science of ACT in an exceptionally practical and easy to read way. He will teach you how to apply the tools and techniques of the ACT model, to not only survive, but actually thrive in your professional life. If you are a medic working in healthcare, this book is an absolute must read.

Dr Joe Oliver
PhD PG Dip Clin Psyc
Consultant Clinical Psychologist
Associate Professor
University College London
Founder of Contextual Consulting and co-author of 'The Mindfulness and Acceptance Workbook for Self-Esteem'

This book is a genuinely interesting and compelling read, written from the heart and presented in plain, accessible language. It is a balanced and thoughtful delve into the reasons why we as humans react to adversity and stress in the way we do – and how we can overcome it. It is educative and draws on a meaningful amalgamation of well-used and respected ideas from Education, Psychology, Social Science and Medicine.

Professor Marcus Grace
BSc MSc PhD PGCE CSciTeach FRSB
Professor of Science Education
University of Southampton

Contents

What, why and who?	8
What is going on in my head?	11
What is Acceptance and Commitment Therapy?	13
Understanding the incomprehensible	19
The ACT Hexaflex	29
Summarising ACT	66
In memorandum	73
Where to find help	74
Further reading	75
References	76
Acknowledgements	78
Appendix	80

What, why and who?

Welcome.

You may have opened this book out of curiosity – or with a mind laden with doubt, fear, grief, self-hatred, scepticism, cynicism or maybe even desperation.

Whatever your state of mind, please – read on. Help is at hand.

The world of medicine we work in is a long way from the medical universe portrayed in popular culture. It is hard, even brutal, demanding, exhausting and challenging, and we as healthcare professionals are NOT angels or saints. We are ordinary human beings, often called upon to do extraordinary things. The day-to-day work of healthcare may create or intensify difficult feelings until, at its lowest ebb, life itself may seem pointless.

Whether you have simply had a bad day or have reached a point where carrying on seems impossible, this book is designed to help you. ACT (pronounced as the word "act") stands for Acceptance and Commitment Therapy. It is a branch of behavioural psychology with the potential to broaden your views of the world and enable you to accept your mind for what it is. Come on a journey with me and start to build the protective mechanisms that will help you lead a richer, fuller and more meaningful life.

Why did I write this book?

I am not a psychiatrist or an expert in psychotherapy, and make no claims to be so. I am a doctor, reaching the end of my training. I was moved to write this after experiencing the impact of ACT on my own life, in the hope it might have a similar impact on yours.

At the lowest point in my life I was in the middle of my training, I had passed my exams and was well regarded by my peers. I had a beautiful wife and child, a supportive family and no problems at home – from an outside view I had everything.

Yet despite this, I was struck with the futility of medicine, overwhelmed with anger and dispassion at a system that seemed designed to irritate and belittle me as a clinician and a person. I was bitter, miserable, and I wanted out. I discussed it with my wife, rewrote my CV, and gave myself six months to get my affairs in order before resigning. At the start of those six months, I referred myself to my local professional support unit, where I was given the opportunity to undergo some therapy. I begrudgingly accepted the offer.

This was my first experience with ACT, and it has changed the entire way I look at life. With an understanding of *how* and *why* our minds can make us so unhappy, even in happy situations, and given the tools to deal with this, I have rediscovered joy in my life and work.

However outwardly successful and happy you may appear, no-one is immune to feelings of self-doubt, anger and despair. But however disillusioned and battered you are feeling, you are not alone – and there IS a way through.

Who is this book for?

This book is designed as a quick, easy-to-read guide to improving your psychological outlook and helping you cope with the stress of day-to-day life. It is specifically written to appeal to those with medical training, offering an in-depth view of the therapeutic goals of ACT and providing examples tailored to everyday scenarios within medicine.

It is a companion read, deliberately pared down to the basics and light enough to carry in a bag to hospital or clinic. There is no pressure to read this book cover-to-cover, or in one sitting. If you want to stop reading, don't be afraid to close the book and put it down. It will always be there for you whenever you need it.

I have used the following features to make it easier to navigate the ideas presented in this book, and to help you find the pathway most helpful to you.

> **Important ideas** are written in blue boxes. These offer key points of understanding about ACT and how we think

> **Exercises** are written in green boxes. These offer psychological tools designed to focus you on key elements of ACT

> **Examples** are written in yellow boxes. These are specific examples of how exercises or concepts of ACT can be applied to your practice

Read on to learn more about how your mind works, how medicine can force us into narrowed views that are detrimental and unhelpful, and what we can do to prevent it.

What is going on in my head?

Within medicine we are constantly taught to look for scientific evidence; we review, weigh up, and categorise to diagnose physical illnesses and administer the best treatment. This rigorous attitude makes it is all too easy for us to believe that our view of the world is infallible – and the only one. We tend to be sceptical if psychology is mentioned. But our minds are incredibly powerful tools, and just as we think our world view is objective, balanced and reasonable, so too does every one of our colleagues, patients and loved ones. It is worth recognising the incredible variation in personalities, opinions and biases around you every day. The actions of each and every person are justified in their own mind.

To help illustrate the power of the mind, take a few minutes to immerse yourself in the following exercise.

> Sit down in a quiet, private space and take a deep breath.
>
> As you breathe, focus.
>
> Imagine someone you love, someone who is or was very close to you – your partner, your child, your parent or your friend – someone important in your life. Think of all they mean to you, the times they have supported or loved you. Focus on them sitting in a simple white room, with no windows, doors or shelves, just white walls and the white chair on which they sit.
>
> Now imagine that person in quiet, deep sorrow. Focus on their face, their tears as they form and roll down their cheeks. Imagine their shoulders as they hunch over in grief, alone.
>
> While you picture this scene, pay attention to your thoughts and feelings. Do you want them to stop? Do you want to help them? Do you want to know why they are crying? Do you feel sad yourself? Do you feel angry or manipulated into thinking about something upsetting?
>
> Whatever your thoughts and feelings, they are directed at an imaginary scenario. You are grieving, angry or sad at a scene that has never been and never will be. This is just one small example of the power of the mind, and how we can harness it – with both positive or destructive results.

No matter what your role in the healthcare system – whether hundreds of people obey your every whim or you are the most junior of trainees – we all live in a universe entirely within our own heads.

Our reality is based on thoughts and feelings which are themselves based on everything we have experienced in our lives. Our mind clearly recalls happy faces, beautiful sunsets, tender moments, pinnacles of achievement. But with equal ease it has the power to create unparalleled pain and suffering.

ACT shows you how to accept and embrace the power of your mind, developing and practicing skills which enable you live a richer and more fulfilling life.

What is Acceptance and Commitment Therapy?

Acceptance and Commitment Therapy is, first and foremost, an empirically based intervention shown to increase psychological flexibility – vital for all healthcare workers in their work, and for personal well-being for everyone.

ACT helps you

- identify the core values that really matter to you
- recognise and defuse intrusive or unhelpful thoughts
- make the most of each moment

Within psychology, objective data remains challenging to gather – something that, rightly or wrongly, can raise a feeling of scepticism within medicine. Some studies in ACT look at familiar statistics such as survival, readmission rates, drug dose reductions and so on – 'hard science', if you will. Others rely on assessments using psychological wellbeing scores. It is easy to dismiss this as 'soft science' – but many of these scores are based on well-validated and rigorously studied tests. There are hundreds of publications carefully reviewing and assessing the utility of these assessments with the same scientific rigor we apply to any therapy or scoring systems within medicine. These scores are used within many medical papers, such as COSMIC-EOL – a randomised multi-centre trial published recently in the Lancet – which utilised questionnaires to quantify grief in the bereaved relatives of critical care patients. They are used within academic medicine for wellbeing studies on patients with cancer and other chronic disease to gauge all-important quality of life years. It would be rash, therefore, to dismiss them in their role in psychology.

There have been hundreds of studies looking at the effectiveness of ACT in a variety of patient populations, many focussing on depression and anxiety, but others on other psychological or psychiatric conditions including Obsessive Compulsive Disorder, Borderline Personality Disorder, Schizophrenia and Bipolar Affective Disorder.

The vast majority of these studies demonstrated a statistically significant improvement in scores for mood, depressive symptoms and wellbeing in patients receiving ACT psychotherapy, not only over placebo but also over other interventions. In 2015, 2019 and 2020 there were three large meta-analysis studies focussing on ACT, reviewing thousands of participants, which found ACT to be effective therapy compared to placebo and standard care for a wide variety of conditions and scoring systems for wellness. Other studies have demonstrated significant improvement in relapse or readmission rates for patients with psychiatric pathology after only a few focussed sessions of ACT.

ACT won't help everyone – nothing will – but if you are struggling with the stress of your professional role or with issues beyond the workplace – this is an empirically proven intervention to try.

The bare bones of the idea

Professor Steven Hayes was one of the creators of ACT from work based on a novel concept of linguistic and cognitive processing known as *Relational Frame Theory* (RFT). This theory argues the main building block of human language and cognition is the ability to create untrained bidirectional links between objects and concepts.

From the moment we develop our rudimentary cochlear we are bathed in words. Even within the womb we are exposed to our parents' voices, which only become clearer and more important as we are born and grow.

As toddlers, we are handed objects and given their names; a cup, a ball, a plate. We are trained in the relationship between the name and the object. This is initially similar to animals, who can be trained to appreciate unidirectional links in simple associative learning. A dog will respond and have a concept of a 'biscuit' but will not be able to make the conceptual link to all 'treat' or 'reward' stimuli. Conversely, a very young child will recognise that a 'cup' is not just a single object, but a range of different objects that they, and others around them, use for drinking.

If you hand a three-year-old a rubber duck and call it a "duckie", they will be able to identify other rubber ducks that are *not* the original as a "duckie" as well, *despite* not being trained in this and with differences in shape, size and orientation. This is an untrained, bidirectional relationship between the object's *concept* and *function*. RFT hypothesises that this conceptualisation is the key to our language development and our ability to form cognitive links between unrelated events or objects.

Relational frame theory is far more complex than the simplified version above, but the complexities of language processing and the concepts of behavioural linguistics are thankfully not necessary to understand or use ACT. If you are interested in the detailed history of ACT, and its roots in behavioural psychology and RFT, have a look at the work of Professor Steven Hayes or 'ACT made simple' by Dr Russ Harris.

Figure 1. A child can develop conceptual links to new objects via untrained relational processes that correlate key aspects of that object to previous stimuli

In the figure above, at an early developmental stage we have the ability to relate objects by characteristics including their size, shape, colour, position and location. Humans alone possess the ability to relate such vastly complex relationships to concepts that live only within our mind. Take the example below; the word 'dog' compared to an actual dog and the written version of the word.

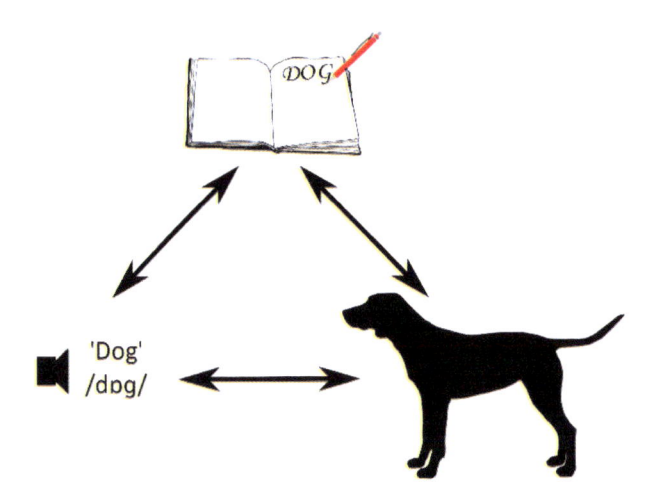

Figure 2. The conceptual framework of a dog; the written word, the spoken name and the visual cue. All of these summon the essence of a dog into our mind, despite the physical absence of any canine.

All three things *mean* dog, and we are able to comprehend and understand that, despite there not being any *real* dog in the vicinity of the page.

If we take this a step further, we realise that our minds relate each object not only with the *concept* of the object but also our subjective *opinion* of the object based on our knowledge, thoughts, feelings, memories, biases and subconscious judgements. You may have felt delighted at the idea of a dog, or immediately thought of a beloved pet – but if you have an allergy to pet hairs, or have been bitten, maybe your feelings were less enthusiastic. Even if you have never met a dog before, these conceptual links mean you can *still* feel anxious if you have been told that dogs bite or are dangerous.

All of these internal processes together are, according to RFT, the framework of how our mind creates and views our internal reality, through an almost infinite web of bidirectional connections linking everything you see and hear with the individual concept of 'you'. With no prompting or conscious thought, our minds create two-way links to everything we experience.

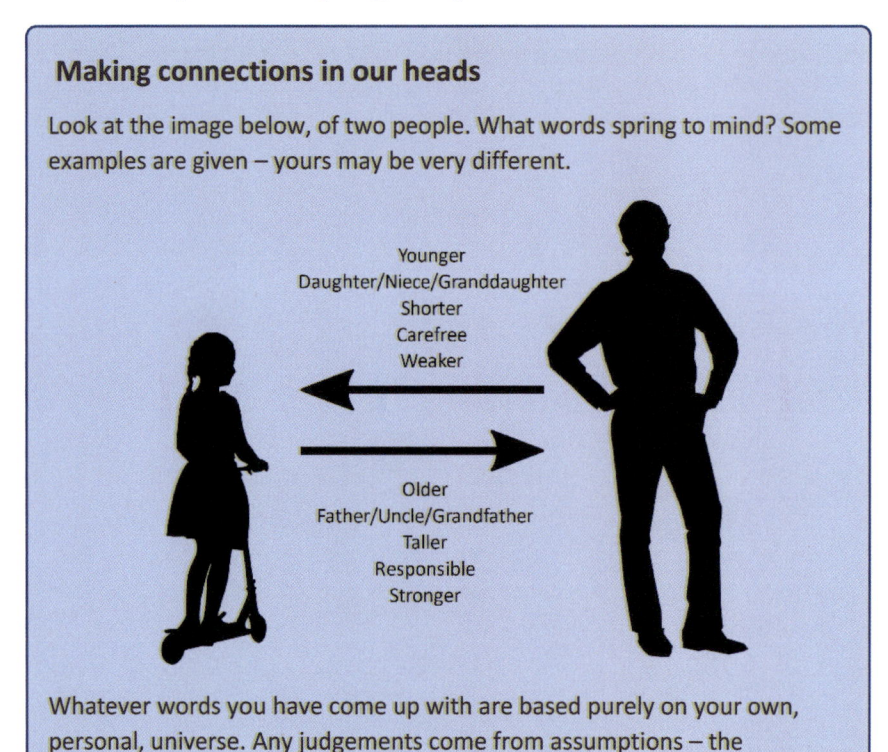

Making connections in our heads

Look at the image below, of two people. What words spring to mind? Some examples are given – yours may be very different.

Younger
Daughter/Niece/Granddaughter
Shorter
Carefree
Weaker

Older
Father/Uncle/Grandfather
Taller
Responsible
Stronger

Whatever words you have come up with are based purely on your own, personal, universe. Any judgements come from assumptions – the perspective, the apparent clothing, the assumed gender.

You may feel slightly sceptical about RFT or the logical steps taken to expand on it in routine psychology. It is admittedly hard to gather solid evidence of how it functions within the discipline of neurophysiology, and there is a great deal of controversy about it even within psychology, but there is a wealth of evidence supporting it as an innate and powerful tool in learning and speech therapy. Interestingly, there is strong evidence of success using these techniques in children with autism, helping them form mental connections to improve emotional and language comprehension.

How humans differ

Many other species of animals possess songs, sounds and body postures for communicating with others of their kind, but however complex the communication system, they lack the finesse, specificity and creativity that singles out humanity.

This was of significant interest to many researchers from the 1950s to the 1980s, leading to some bizarre and unethical experiments. Animals such as dolphins and chimpanzees were reared with significant human contact or even in human families, in an attempt to see if language "rubbed off" on them. These experiments demonstrated some tragic aspects of mammalian emotional intelligence and the deep bonds that animals *can* form, especially when these research families were separated. But none of this research produced a literate ape or talking cetacean.

Some primates, such as Koko the Gorilla, have been taught rudimentary sign language, but the extent and understanding of their grasp of language remains heavily debated. Chimpanzees can memorise words or numbers and their order – in fact they have a strikingly better memory for recalling the location and order of figures than humans. The limiting factor in all other animal species is the lack of demonstrable *understanding* of language and literacy.

Evolutionarily we know that as our frontal lobe began its rapid development and growth, we also evolved socially into structured tribes. It would have been impossible to maintain the numbers of people found in these tribes with only the rudimentary communication seen in other apes. The drive for language and social understanding may have selected for brains adept at forming these bidirectional links. The processing and neuronal connections required to make these links were also gigantic, driving the evolution of our large, characteristic, frontal lobe. It is, as said, merely a theory, but there is some convincing evidence in its favour.

RFT hypothesises that the ability to make links between apparently unrelated objects is the key skill we humans possess, and other animals do not. Our success as a species relies on the potentially unique ability we have to *relate* to the world around us. This is beneficial in so many ways. We hear and understand order and consequence, we can plan and imagine events in distant time and space, we recognise when others are hurt, we reach out and appreciate connections in a way no other organism can – but it comes at the price of incredible psychological vulnerability. The links occur in both directions – just as we recognise someone else's pain, we ourselves are influenced by it. We have an empathetic mind. Subconsciously or not, we interpret and create our reality based on the world around us.

If, as in healthcare, our surroundings routinely involve disease, mortality, pain, suffering and death, it is little wonder we are at such a risk of psychological distress and burnout. This is the price we often pay for our empathetic minds – but it is NOT inevitable. There are ways we can recognise, neutralise, and equalise our own propensity to absorb hurt. Picking up this book is your first step in becoming more aware of your own mental processes and understanding how you can train them to lead a richer and more fulfilling life.

If you have picked up this book, you have recognised that you need help – so where is it? There are two ways you can continue to read this book;

> If you want better understanding of **how** our brains work and **why** we end up feeling the way we do; **read on**. This background knowledge can make the next steps more intuitive for some.
>
> Others simply want to get stuck in to changing their life for the better. If that sounds like you, skip to **page 29** to go straight to **The ACT Hexaflex**.

Understanding the incomprehensible – looking into the human mind

There are branches of psychology which discuss the most basic parts of our psyche – the "monkey mind" or "lizard brain" that governs our basic needs and desires such as food and sex. Despite multiple experiments, the 'triune brain' does not hold up under either anatomical or evolutionary examination as a sound model of our evolved mind. A recent study in particular has identified core neuronal types (via transcription factor similarities) which are present throughout the cortex and subcortical regions in both mammalian *and* reptile brains. Even if cursory examinations of the gross anatomy suggest an 'ancient' brain versus our evolved frontal lobe, it fails to appreciate the anatomical or evolutionary complexities that dominate neuroscience.

Recognising which basic drives compel us in our habitual routines or traits doesn't help us accept or understand our more complex thoughts and feelings. So we won't be focussing on these aspects of the brain – instead, we'll focus on the *environment* that drove the development of this brain in our ancestors.

Developing on the Savannah, our early primate ancestors lived in a harsh and dangerous world, where resources were scarce and predators many. This was the background to the evolution of our complex brains. Our thoughts and feelings reflect a brain that needed to constantly identify problems to survive. The hangover of this is a neural network that has multiple deeper structures dedicated to fear, avoidance and reward, and a psychological propensity to identify problems, even when these problems do not exist!

The human mind is complex and multifaceted. One way to consider our evolving psychology is to use four separate concepts, each described as a 'mind'. A 'mind' is differentiated from a 'brain' by being a non-physical concept of thoughts and feelings rather than an anatomical region within the skull. All four of these 'minds' are present in everyone and active at all times, although sometimes one dominates over another. These minds helped our ancestors survive and thrive on the plains of Africa, but they function with the same enthusiasm in the modern world, where they are not always so useful. By identifying and recognising them, we can begin to develop control over them.

The relative mind

The relative mind focusses on the links between objects, people and concepts. These bidirectional links allow us to create, to communicate, to form relationships and to imagine unknown worlds. These links, however, rely on our previous experience – and may influence our future behaviour, either subconsciously or consciously. Even the simplest of sights, actions or phrases is linked by our minds to experiences we've had before – sometimes to our benefit, but sometimes exactly the opposite.

How does this hurt us?

The ability to form bidirectional links can harm those of us working in medicine through the long-term exposure to suffering we see on a daily basis. We connect and form bonds with our patients by sharing in their suffering, but ultimately carry with us a fragment of that pain as we continue on in life. Bear this in mind with colleagues and yourself when you attend an emergency or face a harrowing case.

Our ability to make links is based on our previous experiences – and in medicine this can be both a blessing and a curse – for example, when we meet a clinical scenario that we have seen before, with a similar patient.

> *Example 1*:
> Our previous experience allows us to make a rapid, correct judgement based on our ability to create a connection;
>
> *"These two patients have similar history and blood results, so there is a good chance their diagnosis will be the same"*
>
> *Example 2*:
> Our previous experience acts as a source of bias, judgement or distress;
>
> *"The last patient who presented with an overdose was horrible to me, this one will be the same"*

Our minds are so perfectly able to create these links that we often don't recognise what we are doing until we stop and think. The relative mind is a powerful aspect of our ability to connect emotionally and professionally with our work, but with significant caveats.

The coveting mind

In our harsh past, resources meant survival – food and shelter were essential and scarce. As we see in Maslow's hierarchy of needs, once our basic biological requirements for food, water, sleep and sex are met, the human mind constantly searches for more. Often, more is never enough.

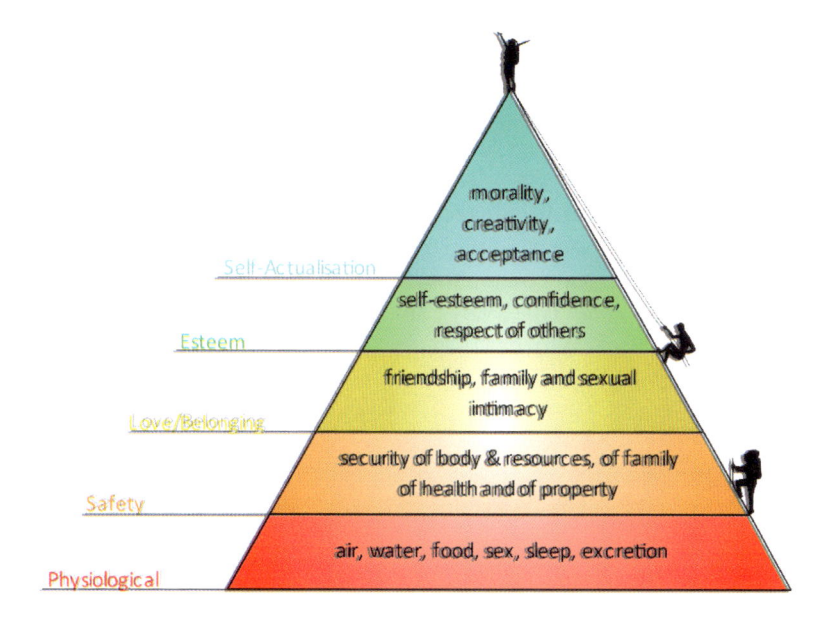

Figure 3. Maslow's hierarchy of needs

In Maslow's hierarchy we require the needs of the layer below to be met before considering the needs in the layer above. Once we have those needs fulfilled, however, we will continue to ascend the pyramid in search of more and more fulfilment.

Eventually, when we reach the summit, "what a [person] *can* be, they *must* be." Self-Actualisation describes the freedom to express and be the person that we feel we are, to behave and act towards values that we hold as intrinsic to ourselves. This is individual to us and, interestingly, is a key part of the core process of *values*.

The impact of the coveting mind is clear; even with our current modern lifestyle, and privileges beyond the imagining of previous generations we are evolutionarily bound to seek out more and more. Perhaps this is contributing to the fact that, despite all we have, psychological issues and difficulties with mental well-being are more prevalent than ever before. It is great to constantly search to better ourselves – but only if this is not at the expense of others or of our own comfort and mental health.

How does this hurt us?

We are assailed every day by adverts and messages telling us we need more physical objects to be truly happy – and it's a very easy message to believe.

In medicine we work long hours for relatively low financial remuneration, if we take into account the actual time worked and how unsocial the hours often are.

We look outside medicine and see our friends and family, who are not working night shifts and long days, who have time to spend and enjoy the money they earn, and who are able to arrange family holidays and plan Christmases without being beholden to a rota.

It is all too easy to become bitter, wrapped up in the idea that everyone else in society, from those in office jobs to lawyers, dentists and refuse collectors, has an easier time of life than we do.

In some ways that's true. The fact is that no one should stay in medicine for financial reward – if you want money, there are other careers which would deliver more. And most of us don't need as much money as we think we do. We can live and be happy with less if it brings mental and physical well-being.

You do NOT have to stay in medicine

This statement comes with a warning – the coveting mind is fickle. Many people in jobs with more free time, or regular hours, look at those of us working in medicine with respect and envy for the prestige and status that still comes with our role in society – and for the salary which, whilst it can feel a poor reward for the toll our work takes upon us, is nevertheless more than most people will ever earn. Envy is a two-way street, and the coveting mind ensures that there will always be an element of someone else's life that you wish to possess.

Leaving medicine will NOT NECESSARILY make you happier. Try ACT as a way to help you in making that decision.

The tribal mind

Archaeological evidence of our human tendency to form social groups dates back around 2 million years. By living together, early hominins shared the labour, gave each other added protection from predators, and provided support between group members. Our social needs have given us many useful psychological skills – but also some difficult baggage. We are very quick to judge others as inside or outside of our particular 'tribe'. Perhaps most damagingly of all, we are quick to judgement of ourselves.

Dunbar's number is 150 – this is the theoretical limit to the number of individuals the human brain can form meaningful relationships with. Acquaintances and people you just about recognise stretch to about 1,500 – but for close relationships 150 is the number found consistently in people and primates. This is of course a crude analysis of modern human cognitive ability, but it is remarkable that Dunbar's number appears in the apparent maximal size of neolithic tribes, settlements and military units globally across history.

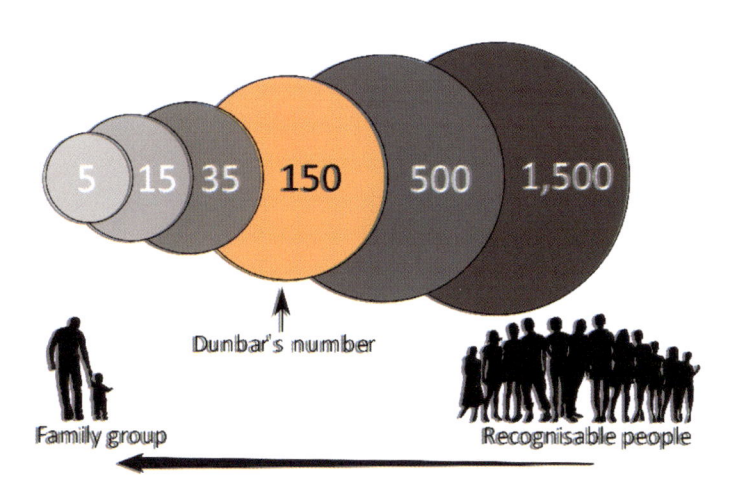

Figure 4. Dunbar's number

150 people in a lifetime has been fine for hundreds of thousands of years – but in modern society 150 may be the number of people we speak to in a day – and that's without tweets and retweets....

The arrival of the internet and social media presents an enormous psychological challenge for the modern mind. On a daily basis we consider, relate and compare ourselves with the maximal number of relationships we evolved to form in a lifetime – and more. No wonder we find life stressful!

How does this hurt us?

Medicine is rife with tribal culture. The profession itself is a tribe, set apart from those following other careers. All of us working in medicine, from the consultants and senior nurses through the juniors and trainees to the receptionists, porters and cleaners, see sights that no-one else could imagine – and we see them on an almost daily basis.

Within medicine there are further tribal divisions between specialties – surgery vs. medicine, GP vs. hospital, clinical vs. management… the list is endless. This makes us feel part of a team and provides camaraderie, but also brings the danger of exclusion, judgements and the concept of *in* and *out* group thinking. This is not novel within medicine – it raises its head in business, sport and culture as well. Becoming aware of this tendency in ourselves allows us to make the most of our natural desire to belong, while recognising and avoiding the potential for alienation and preconceived judgements.

The fearful mind

A distracted mind is a dead mind on the Savannah. Our minds are never quiet, constantly awaiting and expecting great danger around every corner.

This visceral fear is not usually overtly or obviously present in our everyday life and work in UK healthcare situations. But the same instinct, the same constant awareness of danger, presents as problem solving or – more importantly – problem *finding*. In modern life this constant search for problems will inevitably find them – a bill that slipped your mind, an email you forgot to answer, an Insta post you didn't respond to – and your brain interprets this in the same way as seeing the tracks of a lion. It presents many emotions and thoughts; anxiety, distractibility, fear, stress, irritation, anger and more, all produced by a mind evolved to be both uniquely brilliant at problem solving and fearful of the very problems it must solve.

How does this hurt us?

Medicine is full of stressful decisions, and the repercussions of these decisions. Our minds are excellent at seeking out and finding these insecurities – and dwelling on them. Everyone is familiar with a sleepless night after leaving an unstable patient, or the worry that can plague us after a difficult shift. We relive the brusque remark from a consultant, we fret over the comments of a family hurt, stunned and angry when they discover their loved one isn't just going to get better, we go over and over the rude, aggressive, drunk, drugged patients who have been physically and verbally abusive to us as we try to help them, and plan what we wish we had managed to say...

Psychology within medicine

There are hundreds of studies exploring the different psychological profiles of nurses, doctors, surgeons, paramedics and all the subspecialties within our healthcare family. While characteristics and stereotypical behaviours may differ between groups, in reality our minds remain remarkably similar. Our shared evolution and the basis of our thoughts and feelings remain unchanged. It is remarkable that different attitudes and beliefs produce such wildly different behaviours between individuals, when our brains function on almost exactly the same neural programming.

The expectation within medicine – and within the general public – is for us to be professional, courteous – and faultless.

This is understandable. We are in a position of great responsibility and privilege and have the potential to do great harm as well as great good.

But we are human, and humans cannot be professional, courteous and faultless all the time, or even most of the time. Each of us has relative, coveting, tribal and fearful minds, as do our patients – but we are held to far higher expectations than most. We should not be surprised at the high levels of dissatisfaction and burnout within medicine, for we are effectively expected not to think, feel and react as humans have evolved to do.

But while we cannot ignore our evolutionary minds, we can understand them. If we look at the different aspects of our minds, we can see where common pitfalls occur in medicine and how these processes can hinder both our care for our patients and, even more importantly, our care for ourselves.

And once we have recognised the pitfalls, we can set about protecting ourselves from their dangers.

Evolutionary mindsets and medicine

Taking all four concepts of evolutionary minds together and viewing them on an individual level gives us a helpful image of why the modern world is so stressful.

Relative mind
We relate and therefore compare ourselves to people every time we interact

Tribal mind
We value our tribal structure

Coveting mind
We are indirectly (or directly) competing with everyone else for resources

Fearful mind
If we underperform, we are vulnerable to judgement and exclusion

> In summary;
>
> **We judge ourselves based on everyone we meet as if they are one of the 150 people within our tribe. Any area where we underperform compared to anyone we meet therefore makes us feel lesser and vulnerable.**

Considering the number and variety of people we interact with on a day-to-day basis in healthcare, it is inevitable we will underperform compared to *someone*. Our brain interprets this as a personal failing, which in turn we feel damages our reputation within the tribe. We are constantly assuaged by feelings of 'not being good enough' or being an imposter.

IT IS NORMAL TO FEEL THIS WAY

The first thing and most important thing to recognise about the thoughts and ideas we have been looking at is that;

THIS IS NORMAL!

The human mind – your mind – has evolved to be difficult, to maximise your chances of survival in a very different environment to modern life, and modern healthcare.

Now we will explore how to

- accept our mental processes
- clarify what truly matters to us
- use our minds to lead us to a richer, fuller and more meaningful life

<u>This</u> is where ACT comes into its own!

The ACT Hexaflex

The concept of ACT is shaped around six core processes, all of which interlink and complement each other. The **Hexaflex** refers to the hexagonal shape that visually represents these six processes.

When we take these processes on board and practice them, it has been demonstrated that our psychological flexibility improves – and along with it, our mental well-being.

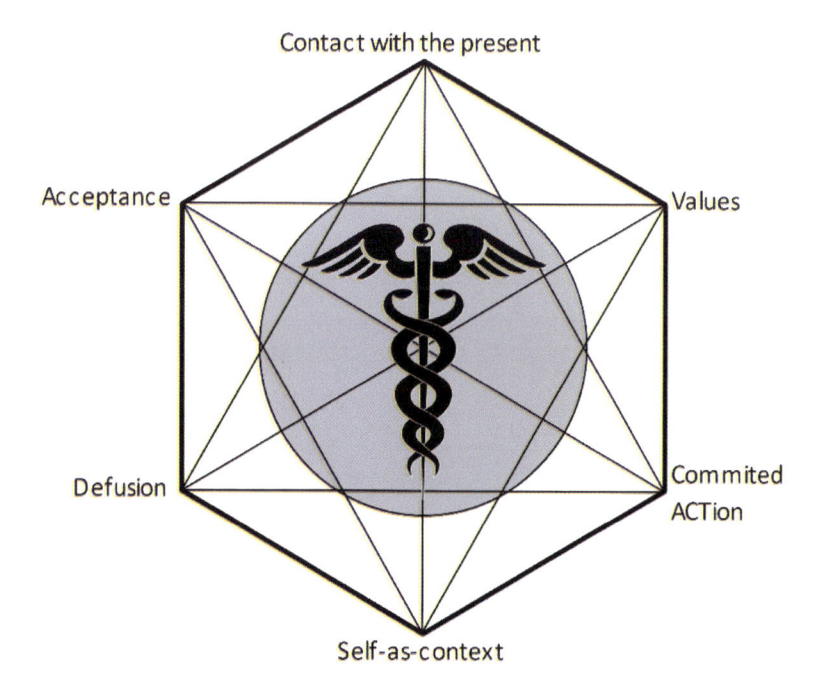

ACT focuses totally on you and the world in YOUR head. Let's explore these six processes in turn, along with their antitheses, and see how they often present within our world of healthcare.

Each process is supported by some imagery, or an exercise to try, along with some common examples – illustrating how easily these processes fit into your everyday practice.

Core process - acceptance

Within ACT, acceptance does not mean being accepting of others or of the world. It is focussed on accepting our own thoughts and feelings as a normal and unchangeable aspect of life. We may still act on them, or because of them, but their ability to overwhelm or bother us is neutralised.

Each day we have hundreds of thousands of thoughts. Most are fleeting or related to what we are currently doing, others are connected tangentially or not related at all, some may be unhelpful or discordant. Acceptance is accepting that the normal, healthy mind contains all of these thoughts – and not fighting to either suppress or hold onto them.

> ### Antithesis: avoidance
>
> The opposite of acceptance is avoidance (formally called experiential avoidance). This is the ongoing attempt to get rid of or avoid the intrusive or unhelpful thoughts that occur naturally and normally within everyday life. This may be helpful initially – it's entirely possible to distract ourselves from these thoughts – but by avoiding them we never grow with them, nor do we grow used to the process of accepting having these thoughts. As soon as one invasive feeling or thought is suppressed another will surface, for that is the nature of the human mind.
>
> Exposure to a stimulus is the basis of almost all psychological interventions. If a patient has a fear of an animal, or heights, then slow and measured exposure to that trigger allows a process of desensitisation and habituation. If the patient continues to avoid these stimuli, there is no possible way of this occurring.
>
> In the extreme case, we will avoid situations and circumstances that trigger difficult thoughts and feelings. This may even involve leaving medicine altogether, abandoning a career we love because we are unable to accept a thought or feeling we dislike.

Opening up and allowing yourself to experience less pleasant thoughts that come into your mind may seem daunting. These negative thoughts may be memories, feelings, emotions, urges, images or impulses that you feel you would rather suppress, or *should* suppress – but the point of ACT is that you don't need to.

The human mind is imperfect and, as we have seen, has evolved to generate difficult thoughts, no matter how hard you try not to. No psychological therapy or input has ever succeeded in negating or stopping this process, but ACT has successfully demonstrated a mechanism to decrease the distress these thoughts can cause.

These thoughts are different for each of us. Perhaps they are of a difficult case or a traumatic cardiac arrest you attended, perhaps they are of your own perceived inadequacy in your job, perhaps they are of future worries about your career, or an upcoming presentation, or coroner's appearance. With any of them, accept that these thoughts are normal, let them occur and allow your consciousness to flow with them.

> Common examples of intrusive thoughts that healthcare professionals experience can include;
>
> - *Thoughts of inadequacy*
>   *I'm not good enough / I don't care enough / I can't do this*
> - *Memories of traumatic events*
> - *Feelings of despondency*
> - *Anger or frustration at faults within the system*
> - *Sensation of being trapped in a place / career / event*

You are not alone in these thoughts

These thoughts are not bad – they are just thoughts

The stream of consciousness

If negative or difficult thoughts, feelings or emotions appear in your mind, the first thing you probably try to do is push them out, not think about them or attempt to think about something else. The reality is that these thoughts will always be flowing through your consciousness.

It's like wading against the current in a river – no matter what effort you put in, the river will effortlessly push you back, and always keep coming.

Your efforts only exhaust you; they don't affect the river at all, nor do they push you further upstream.

Try this...

Find some time, just a few minutes, to sit by yourself – ideally somewhere comfortable but anywhere will do! It may help to close your eyes as you do this. Let your mind wander freely.

Instead of fighting any difficult thoughts or feelings that arrive, just let them come.

Don't focus on them, or try to solve them, or let them lead your mind – just let them go. Simply recognise their arrival and their departure.

It is completely healthy to have these thoughts.

Instead of fighting against the river, you are now turning around and lying back into your stream of consciousness.

Let the current take you with it and float with your thoughts. You will notice that just as they arrived, they will also go – and you won't be exhausted from the fight.

The trapped wolf

Thoughts, constantly flowing through our mind, will contain a variety of themes or content. The most concerning for many of us can be the ones that force themselves into our consciousness, above and ahead of all others. This brand of intrusive thoughts may be distressing and overwhelming and contain the most unpleasant concepts.

These intrusive narratives may even include our brain encouraging us to take the worst and most extreme of actions;

Turn the wheel, drive off the road
Take those drugs
Put your hand into the flame

It is, of course, vital to differentiate these intrusive thoughts from true suicidal ideation.

If you are experiencing constant, coordinated plans of harming yourself, please immediately turn to the section on 'Where to find help' on page 74

When we reach the deepest depths of our despair, when our humanity seems ripped from us and our lives themselves seem useless and hopeless, our brains still seek an answer. Their primary duty remains to seek out problems and solve them.

They attempt to find a solution that will remove us from the situation we are in. The situation is unpleasant, it is uncomfortable, it is distressing.

Our mind attempts to find how we can escape it. Unfortunately, in such situations our issues tend to be multifactorial and fragmented, spread out and difficult to easily define...

Our brains are unable to find an easy solution to remove the problem and so they create the only other answer that they can; remove ourselves from the scenario.

A wolf caught in a trap will attempt everything it can to escape. It will tug, pull and dig at its tether until it bleeds. With each unsuccessful attempt it becomes more distressed, more in pain, more desperate. This is our brain at its lowest moment. In the end the wolf thinks only of escape, gnawing its own leg to the bone in an attempt to remove itself from its situation. In exactly the same way, our brains find the only solution to our despair is to remove ourselves entirely from a world that has become too painful to cope with. Your brain is merely acting as a wolf in a trap, displaying the only solution it can compute that removes all of the stress and worries that assail you.

Recognising *why* these intrusive thoughts occur and accepting that they can be a normal part of psychological stress is an important aspect of self-care. It can be distressing when these thoughts appear, **but by accepting and being prepared for them, you decrease the distress they cause**.

Allow them to drift through your flow of consciousness without driving you to the depths of despair.

Recognise the thoughts for what they are and what they represent, and know that you don't have to gnaw off your own leg to escape the trap.

Examples in medicine

Thoughts occur at all times of our waking life, and while recognising these thoughts is important, so too is letting them go.

Example 1:
Whether departing for the morning handover or arriving home after a shift, some of the thoughts that can flash across our mind or sit under the surface might include:

> "I hate my work"
> "I wish I was home"
> "I hope that patient is ok"
> "What will happen today?"

Accept these thoughts for exactly what they are – thoughts. Chatter from your brain's idle processes that should be recognised but not given undue weight. Let them come and go, only lightly touching them with your consciousness. Don't let yourself dwell on them, don't let them drive your emotions and don't let them colour what is actually happening.

Example 2:
After a poor experience it is easy to let thoughts and opinions destroy us, whether it is a failed exam, a difficult cardiac arrest, a complaint or a miserable experience with a patient. Thoughts that often come to the forefront of our mind might include...

> "If I was better that wouldn't have happened"
> "Everyone knows more than me"
> "Why are patients so horrible?"
> "I can't go on like this"

These experiences are common but important parts of our time on this planet. In every life there will be joy and, in contrast, there has to be sorrow. It can feel nihilistic or defeatist to consider sadness or conflict as 'inevitable' but it is a reality of existence that there will always be sadness and loss. The most treasured relationship has to end, death is inevitable, sorrow is inescapable. By accepting that, purely by the process of living, we will experience sadness, we allow ourselves to recognise that these thoughts, however unpleasant, are temporary. Accepting their inevitability lightens their significance and allows us to let them float down the river.

Core process - defusion

Fusion describes a state of inflexible cohesion with our thoughts, feelings and preconceptions. Our consciousness is influenced by everything we have seen, read, watched or experienced; it is therefore very easy to foster the belief that what we *think* is what is *real*.

Defusion is the process where we unpick this commonly held belief – something quite difficult for medical professionals (or anyone else!) to achieve. We are used to believing that what we see and know is objective fact, based on scientific research and our own clinical skill.

Antithesis: fusion

If defusion allows us to remove ourselves from our thoughts and feelings, then fusion is the opposite – where we allow these internal ideas to become our reality. It is important to note that the concept of fusion itself isn't always a bad thing. It entirely depends on the context.

The technically correct term for fusion is cognitive fusion and it describes any state when one is psychologically fixed on a task or process. During surgery it is natural and desirable for a surgeon to be fused with the procedure being performed, during a film it is normal to fuse with the storyline, even daydreaming can be a positive experience with fusion. None of these detract from experiencing life and moving you towards your goals and values, and thus none should be considered detrimental.

Only when it gets in the way of living a rich and meaningful life does fusion become an issue. There may be colleagues you know who exhibit such traits. Is there a consultant, ward sister or surgeon who shouts and demands their own way? Could they be fused with the concept of themselves within a position of power, or being feared? Do you think they would succeed less or be thought of worse if they asked calmly for what they required? Do these people act as if they are living the rich, full and meaningful life they always wanted?

It is important for us to recognise that accepting the fallible nature of the human mind **doesn't** negate our clinical judgement, in fact it may improve it. The point of defusion is to try to separate the internal thoughts and feelings from our conscious mind; to view them fully but hold them lightly, instead of letting them control us.

The easiest way of understanding defusion is often to consider fusion. There are six forms, all of which are common in medicine. You do not need to memorise any of them but reading through them may give some insight into unexpected ways you might be fused to your mind.

Fusion with the past

This allows past behaviours, events or regrets to overwhelm us and control our thoughts and feelings. It may be because we look at the past event poorly and are consumed with consistent regret, rumination, blame or resentment.

It may be that we view the past favourably and are constantly replaying when we felt our lives were better –

> *My career won't recover from that mistake*
>
> *My life was so much better in my previous hospital*
>
> *Why can't I go back to the way things were?*

Both are unhelpful and decouple us from the present moment, our present self and our present life.

Fusion with the future

This refers to focus on future scenarios that dominates thoughts and removes us from the present. It may be based on a fear of uncertainty, a specific event or anticipating future failures before they occur – it may even be based on chasing a life event...

> *Once I finish these exams, I'll finally be happy*
>
> *My life is never going to get better*

Fusion with the conceptualised self

The **conceptualised self** is a term used to describe the person that we think ourselves to be. Fusion with this conceptualised self can be either a fixed **positive** judgement of self –

> *I'm the most senior, don't question me*

or a fixed **negative** judgement of self –

> *I'm less intelligent than my peers*
>
> *I can't do this procedure*

A third option is **over-identification** with a specific label, whether a diagnosis, a belief or a career. By fusing with these labels, we limit ourselves and stifle our ability to learn, enjoy and experience life.

> *I am a diabetic*
>
> *I'm just a student*
>
> *I'm a consultant*

Fusion with reasons

Humans are excellent at rationalising **why** they cannot achieve or do certain tasks. By finding and fusing with reasons we provide an excuse for not making steps towards our goals or values, which often require effort to achieve. Have you ever wanted to do something but thought to yourself;

> *I'm too Y (busy/tired/stressed)*
>
> *X might happen (rejection/poor outcome/ridicule)*

Fusion with these reasons hold us back from achieving and doing things that would otherwise help us lead a more fulfilling life.

Fusion with rules

Rules are important; they allow us to live in a civilised and equal society where people treat each other with respect.

Self-imposed rules, however, often do not live up to scrutiny, and fixation and fusion with these rules is often unhelpful. Examples of these rules are concepts that include commands such as *I must*, *I should*, and *I have to* or polar concepts about life such as *right/wrong/fair/unfair*.

> *I MUST not make mistakes*
>
> *It's UNFAIR that they get to complain at me*
>
> *I SHOULD work harder*

Fusion with any of these unchecked rules is unhelpful and ultimately only influences our own thoughts and feelings. Others cannot see these self-imposed criteria, no matter how strongly they dominate *your* mind.

> A psychologist named Karen Horney described this overwhelming obsession with rules as **"the tyranny of the shoulds"**
>
> Try noting all the times your brain tells you that you **should** or **shouldn't** be doing something today. Maybe it's telling you how you *should* be feeling, maybe it's berating you because you *should* be working, maybe you're being told you *shouldn't* take time to yourself.
>
> Pay attention to your mind during the day – these shoulds and shouldn'ts can surface in the most unusual ways and places and often reflect unwelcome reminders of expectations that are impossible to attain.
>
> Instead of fusing with these *shoulds*, try to identify them and defuse from them with the exercises on pages 42-46.

Fusion with judgements

This is a more general term for inflexibly holding onto judgements we pass on any and all concepts, events, places and people including ourselves, our body and our feelings.

> Imagine you are fused with a conceptualised self-identity as a 'good doctor'.
>
> *I'm a good doctor*
>
> What happens if you make a mistake while being fused with this concept? If you prescribe the wrong medication or don't notice a rising white cell count? You're left with the judgement that you are not a good doctor.
>
> *I'm (not) a good doctor*
>
> If you're not a good doctor, then you're left with nothing.
>
> *I'm ~~a good doctor~~ → I'm nothing*
>
> This is an exaggerated example, but it illustrates how fusion with a concept can leave you unfocussed and adrift, disconnected from your day-to-day self. Such fusion and subsequent distress is well known and demonstrated in people retiring from professional careers, leaving their entire identity behind.
>
> These extreme opinions are all too easy to foster, as doing so can temporarily make us productive and focussed. The issue arises when becoming **fused** with these concepts detracts from our ability to live a full and balanced life. It is impossible to keep up with the demands these considerations place on us and in trying to do so, we only harm ourselves.

The hands as thoughts

This is a classic ACT exercise developed by Dr Russ Harris in 2009. It helps demonstrate how fusion with our thoughts and feelings prevents us from living to our full potential.

You may want to read the whole of the paragraph below before starting.

Find a quiet space and sit with your hands on your knees.

Focus on your breathing and place your hands together like an open book, with palms facing upwards.

Slowly raise your hands over your face so they almost completely cover your eyes.

Look around the room through the tiny gaps between your fingers.

How much of the room can you see?

How easy would it be to do the things that matter to you right now?

If you **had** to keep your hands up and you were asked to look after a patient, could you?

What if you were asked to hold your child? Or play your favourite sport or musical instrument?

Your hands represent your thoughts, feelings and judgements.

When you are fused with them you can't see past them to look at and do the things that actually matter to you.

With this in mind, slowly bring your hands down and place them on your lap. Look at them and around the room.

Would it be easier to achieve the things asked of you before?

Allowing your hands to lower to your lap simulates the act of defusing. Your thoughts and feelings are still there, but they are removed from your focus, separated from your experience of the present.

By defusing from these thoughts and feelings, they haven't gone away, you haven't lost anything, but you can go about your day and do the things that matter to you without them obstructing you and the view of your life.

Noting, naming and neutralising

What can we do about fusion?

The simplest way to deal with fusion is to identify it, categorise it and place it in perspective – otherwise known as noting, naming and neutralising.

The first step is to simply allow yourself to notice your thoughts and feelings as they go through your head. Initially you may need to consciously stop and wait for your mind to calm enough to notice what thoughts you're actually having.

Sit and think about what thoughts arise when you just watch your mind at rest. Some of them may be helpful or neutral, others may look like this;

> *"This is stupid"*
> *"I'm useless"*
> *"I'm wasting my time"*
> *"I'm not good enough"*

As you practice you will be able to do this naturally as thoughts and fusions arise. It may be uncomfortable, but stay with each thought.

Slowly repeat each thought ten times.

When you have noticed and repeated your thought take the next step to name them as they arrive;

> *"I am having the thought that this is stupid"*
> *"I am having the thought I am useless"*

Again, repeat each phrase ten times before moving on to develop this further by neutralising the thought by distancing yourself from it;

"I notice I am having the thought that this is stupid"
"I notice I am having the thought I am useless"

Slowly repeat this phrase ten times.

You will hopefully notice that with each step you gain distance from the thought, it becomes apparent it just that – a thought. It does not define you nor is it a reality.

With practice this exercise will become easier and easier, allowing you to notice, name and neutralise any unhelpful thoughts that occur, even during your day-to-day work, leaving you free to focus on leading a rich and fulfilling life.

Thanking the mind

This exercise has been particularly helpful to me and focusses on specific types of thoughts or feelings that can occur. These more destructive or unhelpful thoughts are often in response to external events or stimuli.

Personal failings, negative interactions or challenging scenarios may make your mind throw up all sorts of negative comments, seemingly just to illicit a reaction;

"Why couldn't you put in that cannula? You're useless!"
"You don't deserve to be here, you're such a fraud"
"How could you miss that diagnosis? Anyone else would have got it"
"Everyone else was studying last night, you're so lazy"

A simple and quick mechanism to defuse from these sudden thoughts is to 'thank' your brain. Do this quickly, simply and with a degree of irreverence.

"You're such an idiot for forgetting that prescription"
        "Cheers, brain, thanks for sharing"
"Well, you can use defusion all you like, you're still shit"
        "Good for you, brain, thanks"

This rapidly removes the power your thoughts have over your emotions, and defuses these unhelpful interruptions.

It is important to note that you are **not** engaging with your brain in a debate, you are quickly and dismissively thanking your brain for the thought and moving on with your day.

Core process - values

This is one of the most important tenants of ACT. The process of values reflects what truly and honestly matters to **you**. What things in *your* life make it rich, full and meaningful? The most important part of the concept of values is that it must reflect your *own* thoughts and feelings. Your true values should not be affected by anyone else's wishes, expectations or beliefs.

Our values are based on our principles, culture and experiences, and often remain relatively fixed over our lives. The process of discovering our values is one of the more self-reflective elements of ACT, and is often something we have not previously considered in detail. It can therefore take time and self-reflection for you to work out what your core ideals actually are.

Cast your mind back five years – what did you think your life would be like now? What is different? What is the same? Think forward to five or ten years in the future. What does your life look like then?

> ### Antithesis: remoteness from values
>
> It is too easy for what we hold dear to be lost or forgotten when we are wrapped up and fused with our chaotic and disruptive jobs and lives. The point of ACT is to bring our behaviour under the influence of our values, and in doing so lead lives that are more in line with what we hold to be fulfilling and enriching.
>
> Modern medicine is time pressured and unforgiving. Slowly peel away the protective, hedonistic fantasies you have constructed around you in an uncaring world and remind yourself why you wanted to go into medicine in the first place.
>
> Losing sight of our core beliefs, or even just not having time to consider them, can lead us to feel adrift and listless, unfulfilled in our lives and jobs. Sometimes, all it takes is a reminder of what we actually care about to put our lives back into focus and help us realise how we can change what we do to live a life that maximises our experience of the things that truly matter to us.

As we go through our day to day lives and jobs, it is easy to be distracted and lose track of what we value. The idea of holding on to what means the most to us, what we stand for, or how we want to act during our brief time on this planet, is rapidly knocked out of us by the day-to-day frustrations and irritations that come all too easily in healthcare.

At the peak of my despondency, I could only think of one thing: getting out. When my therapist asked me what I wanted my life to look like I said:

> *"Lying on a beach drinking cocktails, forever."*

This wasn't realistic or truly in line with what I valued – it was merely a way to escape. Our brains are experts at problem solving, but when there isn't an easy solution, they throw up answers that are impossible or illogical.

Look at the following short list showing just some of the values that people hold close. It is absolutely ***not*** exhaustive, and the suggestions under each term are only the gentlest of guides. Browse through them and try to pick out the ones which stand out to you.

The list is duplicated in the Appendix at the end of the book. If you want to explore your values more, try cutting these values out as cards and then physically sorting them into separate piles. Think about placing the values into different categories;

- Which ones are not important?
- Which ones are slightly important?
- Which ones are very important?

Once you have these three piles, pick out your top **five** most important values.

Look through these five and select what you feel is your **most** important value.

Don't feel daunted; it's helpful to come back to this exercise a few times to really crystalise what matters to you as an individual.

Take a moment to think about how you can act in your everyday life to maximise bringing this value into your world. Think about how your life would look with more of these values, and how you can take steps every day to bring you closer to this richer, fuller and more meaningful existence.

The ACT Hexaflex

Acceptance To be open and accepting of myself and others	**Assertiveness** To respectfully stand up for my rights	**Authenticity** To be genuine and true to myself	**Beauty** To nurture/create beauty in myself/others
Caring To be considerate and kind to myself/others	**Challenge** To compete to grow, learn and improve	**Compassion** To act with kindness to those who are suffering	**Conformity** To be respectful and obedient to rules/obligations
Cooperation To collaborate and work together with others	**Creativity** To innovate and make or think of things differently	**Curiosity** To be open-minded and want to explore and discover	**Encouragement** To encourage and reward behaviour I value
Equality To treat myself as equal to others and vice versa	**Excitement** To seek/create exciting experiences	**Fairness** To be fair to myself and others	**Fitness** To improve my physical health and wellbeing
Freedom To live freely and be able to choose how I behave	**Friendliness** To be compassionate and agreeable to others	**Fun** To seek/create enjoyable activities	**Humour** To see and engage in the humorous side to life
Humility To be modest or humble	**Industry** To be hard working and dedicated	**Intimacy** To share myself emotionally with those close to me	**Love** To show affection to myself and those I care about
Order To be orderly and organised	**Patience** To wait calmly for what I want	**Pleasure** To create enjoyable things for myself and others	**Respect** To be considerate to others and expect the same back
Responsibility To be accountable for my actions	**Safety** To protect others and avoid accidents	**Sexuality** To express or explore my sexual drive/libido	**Spirituality** To explore or connect with a religion or higher power

Life's a beach

This exercise may help you pinpoint what your values are, by giving your brain the ideal life you may be considering and discovering how well it reflects your true core values.

Find a quiet spot to do this exercise, sit back and think of your escape.

This might be a different job, outside of medicine, it might be an eternal holiday on a beach or a special memory of a perfect moment.

Think about that idealised segment of time. Hold the image in your mind, the one that you quite possibly long to escape to every day, that distracts you from your work and the present moment.

As an example, we will take my fantasy of lying on a beach with a cocktail in hand and toes buried in the warm, white sand. I wanted nothing more than to escape to this idea – I couldn't think of anything else. My therapist made us carefully work through what would change if I brought my values into this fantasy.

This can be any of the values on the list before, manifested as a scenario that highlights the core tenants of that value. 'Caring' or 'Compassion' are good ones to start with.

On this beach, as you lie there, imagine a person walking past. You didn't notice them arrive, but here they are, struggling and limping as they walk past you at the edge of the sea. They are clearly hurt; their face is contorted in pain and they struggle to make each step. What do you think you would do?

This is your perfect moment. You want for nothing and yet, I will wager, for many of you there will be an urge to step forward and help them.

Stepping out of your fantasy and aiding a fellow human demonstrates that you *do* care (at least a little!). You possess compassion and hold it as one of your core tenants – whether you want to recognise that or not. Try this or other scenarios for other values, slowly replacing the person walking by with other situations, exploring each of the values above to find those that resonate with you the most. It might be…

> *Justice* – An unfair argument between two strangers
> *Leadership* – A group who are lost and need a guide
> *Art* – An opportunity to write or paint as the sun sets
> *Curiosity* – An unknown animal crosses in front of you

Examples in medicine

Medicine allows us to explore and fulfil many avenues, but only by focusing on ourselves are we able to recognise what in medicine aligns us to our core values. For many the concept of caring for others is intrinsic to their sense of themselves – as well as part of their dedication to medicine – yet in the tough hurly-burly of health care it is all too easy to lose sight of this. For others it is the challenge of learning or training in a skill or procedure and mastering it that brings them satisfaction.

After doing the exercises above, list what you find important in your life and consider how medicine provides you with that. Are there any changes you could make in your role or your day-to-day life that would better align you with your values?

It may be that you can continue in your role in medicine but regain a focus on other intrinsic values. For example, I had completely forgotten the joy that literature and writing brought me. By refocussing on this I used my spare time to write and draw. The ability to express myself in my free time made me far happier during work, and the experiences I gained in work I used in my writing.

After exploring our core values and refocussing on how our job aligns with them, it is often easier to cope with the challenges of our role in healthcare. Focussing on what in your work brings you closer to what you personally find important can be a major step in rekindling joy in your work and your personal life.

The major caveat to this is that you may explore your core values and find that medicine *doesn't* align with any of them or doesn't align with them enough or in a way you find meaningful. This is an equally valuable insight, as it offers a chance to reconsider your career choices and explore the possibilities of a role or job that *would* align you with your core values.

Core process - self-as-context

To think about this core process, we first need to think about the conceptualised self. Our conceptualised self is the subjective idea we hold about ourselves and the image we think we project onto the world. The opposite of this is our self-as-context, which involves viewing our behaviour and interactions with the world from an objective viewpoint.

But how can we look at ourselves objectively?

We are all familiar with the layers of thoughts that we have on a second-by-second basis, and science is many years away from dissecting exactly how the process of conscious thought occurs. The approach to self-as-context is to differentiate between the consciousness that notices and the thoughts, feelings, sensations and behaviours we generate.

It is as though you are looking at your life from the perspective of another, impartial individual. It removes the backstory, the judgements and the expectations we carry with us and focuses on making you view yourself as you really are.

> ### Antithesis: fusion with the conceptualised self
>
> We have already explored fusion as one of the core processes – remember that any fusion leads to an inflexible and narrowed mindset.
>
> We all have a narrative we tell ourselves about our lives, it's normal and natural to think of ourselves in the context of our upbringing, environment and history. It is only when we become *fused* with a judgement, concept, or idea about ourselves that this becomes problematic.
>
> These judgements can be negative;
>
> > *"I'm not good enough"*
> > *"I always make mistakes"*
>
> However, it is just as possible for fusion to be problematic when these judgements are positive;
>
> > *"I always know best"*
> > *"I don't need help"*

This concept of objective thought is well known to anyone who has practiced or learnt about Buddhist meditation. Indeed, many of the concepts of ACT have been used in religious thought and Eastern philosophy for thousands of years. The process demands we observe ourselves – our actions, our thoughts, our feelings, our emotions – from an external, unjudging and objective view.

Some meditation practitioners take many decades to even get close to doing this consistently, which highlights how challenging it can be for humans to take the vital step back and view ourselves as the objective universe sees us. Do not feel that ACT demands this level of observation and concentration all the time – we all have far too much in our lives to consider this a possibility. Instead, use this skill in key moments to consider how others might be seeing you, allowing yourself to step back from the universe inside your own skull and attempt to view yourself and your actions as the world actually sees them.

The theatre

This is a conceptual exercise to help you understand what self-as-context means. It is not a prescriptive experience nor is it exhaustive, and many branches of meditation and mindfulness have additional methods or visualisation exercises that can help you in visualising self-as-context.

Imagine you are at the theatre, sitting in a seat and looking at the performers on stage.

The stage, the actors, and the scenery all represent you – your thoughts, emotions, and behaviour as you go about your day-to-day life. Watch as they move around your consciousness, how they express themselves to others in your behaviour and actions.

You are not part of it but merely observing, watching at the show playing out in front of you. You can see and appreciate all the nuances and subtleties in the performance, but you're not there to judge it.

That last point is very important – as an outside observer you are simply watching. Let only the objective details filter through to you. Ignore the subtleties and subtext from your past and the chatter of your internal narrative as much as possible.

This is a hard skill to achieve and involves using defusion and acceptance to try to consider only the current, unbiased moment.

This is the way to view yourself when thinking of self-as-context, just watching the entire process spread out in front you of.

Use this concept to consider how you see yourself, and how your patients, your colleagues or your family see you.

To take this a step further, now imagine someone else watching you watching the play. How might they view the way that you view your own thoughts and feelings?

This is a step further towards self-as-context, watching your thoughts as you watch your thoughts. This can be continued indefinitely as a self-reflective exercise to improve and aid in your ability to remove yourself from situations and, without judging, see the context and associations at play behind your mental processes and actions.

Try using this exercise next time you speak to a friend or your partner. Attempt to sit outside your own mind as you observe yourself as you speak. How does it make you feel to watch yourself in action?

Examples in medicine

Within each shift there are a thousand different impressions we make on others, and that others leave on us. These rely on dozens of soft signs that combine to form a general impression, from body language to the subtle stress on a word in a sentence.

Being able to tease apart our own biases and see the moment with objective clarity helps avoid misunderstandings and miscommunications, along with enabling you to present the version of yourself that most aligns with your core values – improving outcomes for yourself, your colleagues and for patients.

Example:
Consider being approached by a colleague from a different specialty with a request. You are busy, and feel the request is outside of your regular duties. It is easy to snap that it isn't your problem, at the very least being brusque and unhelpful, at worst escalating the situation to an argument.

Instead, take that pause and look at the situation from the outside. Your colleague has respect for your opinion, but has no idea how busy you are at that moment. They may not recognise that their request is unreasonable, or maybe it is your stress level that is dictating what is or is not unreasonable? How would you want someone to respond to you if you approached them in the same way? If they *are* being unreasonable, how is the best way to defuse the scenario?

Taking the time to think about how others would see this scenario helps remove our own biases, and with practice it counterintuitively *decreases* our cognitive load – we focus on the objective instead of also having to consider our emotions. This is a very difficult skill to hone in high stress scenarios, so take the time to practice. Maybe use the theatre exercise above to help you consider how to view yourself from an objective viewpoint. Being prepared and practiced will help you remain calm and unbiased as and when a situation arises.

Core process - contact with the present moment

Our minds constantly travel through time, rocketing back and forth between what has been and what will be. This is beneficial, it allows us to plan our lives based on the experiences of our past, and to relive pleasant thoughts and feelings. It does, however, come with the unhelpful side effects of also allowing us to obsess over events that have never happened (many of which *will* never happen) or stay tethered to things which occurred many years ago.

Obsession or focus on either one disrupts our lives in the present. That is not to say that we should **only** focus on the tiny fraction of space-time we inhabit, but rather that we should bear in mind that, for all our consideration of what has been or will be, we live in what currently *is*.

Many meditation and mindfulness programs focus on grounding ourselves in the present, often attempting to maintain this state of mind at all times. Realistically, this is incredibly difficult, especially when so many other things are happening in and around a busy and full life. You may be dealing with a patient in A&E or ITU, or removing an appendix – but that doesn't mean your toddler doesn't have chickenpox, your partner might not be leaving you, you don't have social commitments that evening, you don't have bills that need sorting...

ACT focusses on training your mind to take tiny moments of mindfulness when suitable and possible for your lifestyle, touching base with the present repeatedly within a busy life. There is no demand that you sit still for forty minutes and force yourself to focus. Instead, you are invited to take the luxury of focussing on the here and now for just a few seconds before or after everyday tasks. By fitting mindfulness around your real-life existence, it becomes significantly easier to practice these skills regularly, and therefore easier to improve them.

Antithesis: inflexible attention

Inflexible attention refers to an inability to focus our mind on the present. The human mind normally and naturally focusses on the past and future, to review past strategies and prepare for future dangers. This, like much of the mind, isn't an inherently bad thing, but by losing control of this ability we become unable to focus on what really matters in the here-and-now.

The cause of this inflexible attention often falls into one or more of the 'three Ds'; **distractibility**, **disengagement** or **disconnection**.

Distractibility
Refers to difficulty sustaining attention on tasks or thoughts. The focus shifts to other thoughts or considerations, which makes concentration and grounding far harder. This commonly results in poor performance during our everyday tasks, poor recollection of what we were doing and decreased satisfaction in our day-to-day activities.

Disengagement
Refers to a decrease or lack of conscious connection to our experience of the world. Mindlessly completing tasks on a relative 'autopilot' without engagement or focus.

Disconnection
Refers to an inability to make contact with our thoughts and emotions. For some this may be because they feel uncomfortable when connecting to or thinking about their inner thoughts, or because they feel they don't have to. For others it may be involuntary, as part of a more pathological process such as depression.

The inability to focus and ground ourselves in the present ultimately leads to a less fulfilling experience of life. We can't recognise and enjoy what is happening around us unless we pay attention to and notice each moment as it occurs.

Taking a second

Fit this exercise in and around your daily routine. Start by choosing one thing you do every day: locking your front door, parking your car, cleaning your teeth. The next time you do that activity focus on 'taking a second' and thinking about what you are doing.

Let's use the example of locking your front door.

Next time you are leaving the house, take the time for this exercise. Standing outside your front door, even if you feel the need to hurry, get your key out and **take a second**.

For a *literal second* let your mind focus on the task.

Notice your stance, the temperature and scent of the air around you, the feeling of the ground beneath your feet and the key in your hand. Control your muscles consciously as you turn the key.

As soon as the task is done you can return to your everyday thoughts – don't feel pressured to continue thinking in the present, but you may find that you catch yourself doing it anyway.

In another example let's look *inwards* rather than outwards.

When you're cleaning your teeth, stood in the bathroom before getting into bed at night, allow your body to take over the task and focus on what is happening inside your head. What is your mind thinking about?

Is it ruminating about something that happened during the day? Are there unhelpful thoughts or self-judgements resurfacing? Are you thinking that the bathroom needs renovating?

Let your mind focus and note each thought and feeling as it travels across your mental landscape. After holding this state for just a second or two, relax your concentration and continue with your usual thoughts.

Try extending this exercise as you use it, recognising that some days you will fit in a minute or even five of contact with the present, and others you will be lucky to get a single second.

Once it becomes more natural to you, you may find it helpful to start using these grounding moments in your practice, before the start of a ward round, before a procedure or before presenting a patient.

Take the time, and treat yourself to being grounded and focussed in the present moment.

Examples in medicine

The benefit of this form of mindfulness is that it does not expect or tout the requirement of constant, zen-like concentration. Instead, it attempts to demonstrate how small moments of applying these mindfulness techniques can refocus us in high stress environments or emotive events.

As with any skills, as you practice grounding yourself it becomes an easier and more engrained habit. This allows us to apply this skill when we need it. In medicine, the hectic environment may initially be too distracting for you to make contact with the present moment. By working these exercising into your everyday life you make it far easier to achieve a state of concentration when you need it.

The following examples focus first on how we can use our contact with the present moment to improve our wellbeing, and then how we can use it to improve our clinical skills and performance.

Example 1:
Medicine is exhausting. There are times when it seems like there is no rest, no let up from the constant demands and barrage that assails us as soon as we come on shift. The next time you are at work, or on your way to or from work, try to take that moment. Take a minute, or thirty seconds – it really only has to be that small amount of time. Practice the exercises above, focussing on the things that you might otherwise have missed.

There will be pleasant feelings and sensations along with the unpleasant, but the most important part is making sure you take the time to do it.

Example 2:
Distractions occur all too often in daily life. Engaged in a task such as taking a history, checking patient test results or filling in a form, our minds may wander, becoming focussed instead on how many hours we have left of our shift, whether we need to shop for food for dinner on the way home or a thousand other everyday considerations.

The dangers of inflexible attention are all too real in medicine. The times we drop our attention put us at risk of missing key facts. ACT helps ensure that we take a moment and reflexively collect ourselves before undertaking key clinical skills, thus improving our focus and reducing our chances of missing vital information.

Example 3:
The ability to switch off our conscious mind and undertake tasks on 'autopilot' is a fascinating phenomenon. This lack of engagement can be safe and pleasant, but in our clinical roles it removes awareness of our actions. This in turn potentially increases the risks of making mistakes during procedures or routine duties. Take the time, before a task, to ground yourself, check your equipment and to focus on what you are about to do.

Using this technique before a clinical task, such as siting a cannula or drawing up medicines, allows you to consider what needs to be done, to examine it in depth and to give yourself time to think before approaching the patient. This focus can be invaluable, particularly after practice, as the investment of a tiny amount of time in mindfulness gives renewed clarity and concentration for these tasks during high stress scenarios.

In summary:

We may become detached from our connection with the present due to a lack of interest or to unpleasant events. Some people find little pleasure in considering their own mental processes, while other find it hard because of the unpleasant feelings that arise.

I hope that, by reading this book, some who would otherwise have ignored such techniques see the potential benefits. Utilising these exercises to focus and connect to the present can be beneficial not just psychologically, but in improving our technical prowess as well.

For this reason, ACT is practiced within Olympic teams and businesses, particularly in the United States. There are multiple papers written on using ACT to improve skills and outcomes in sporting events, especially post injury. It has tremendous potential to improve your life experience – and your performance in medicine too.

Core process - committed ACTion

This is the last psychological process of the Hexaflex, and the one that is hardest to both define and perfect. You may have already attempted the exercises in this book, and hopefully found them helpful. Some may resonate with you more than others, and that is where **committed ACTion** begins.

ACT is not a therapy with an end goal where we can stop the course and label it as 'complete' or 'cured'. It is a psychological model to improve wellbeing and performance via the continual use of its elements in your everyday life. ACT is a way of thinking that, with practice, enriches you, builds resilience and helps you lead a more meaningful, value-driven existence.

It may seem daunting at first to consider changing the way you think and process the world, but is it any different from using a glass of wine or a bar of chocolate to unwind in an evening? ACT entails as much or as little input from you as you desire, although obviously the more you engage and practice, the easier it becomes. The aim is not to change you directly, but to improve your ability to cope with change. It may be that you find yourself changing, but in line with your new goal of behaving in a way that aligns with your core values and ideals.

It is worth reiterating along with this that, as with any skill or activity, your ability to use ACT will improve as you practice. It requires patience and consideration when you have the time and headspace, giving you more chance of using it successfully when it is most needed. This can be difficult when we are at our most vulnerable. It may feel daunting to use our precious free time reading and considering mental exercises, however little time they take. But to give yourself the best chance at using ACT successfully, it is worth taking the time to practice it in easy scenarios in your own time before deploying it in the stress of the work environment. This gives you chance to consider your core values, your behaviour, to take a second and feel the world around you when you are in a safe space, before you are in a situation where you have to confront an angry colleague or grieving relative, and need the self-awareness and resilience that ACT gives you.

With practice, your ability to use ACT successfully in challenging scenarios will increase, but never expect it to be perfect. Don't judge yourself if you snap and become angry or act in a way that does not align with your values. It is *normal* and *expected* to find life hard and for our scenarios to sometimes be inescapably stressful, and our responses less than perfect.

The psychological flexibility that ACT offers is designed to not only help you deal with any adversity you are currently facing but also with any crisis in the future. Whatever you decide to do with your life, when there is conflict or strife, the core processes of ACT can help you through it. The key difference is that if you start now, *you will already have practiced these processes before you need them*.

Therapy and ACT are not there to keep you in medicine, and these processes are just as useful if they convince you that you **don't** want to continue. Don't feel guilty if you make the decision that medicine is no longer for you – there are a wealth of resources to help you take that leap into a different career. But if you remain in healthcare, then ACT gives you the power to get the most out of your **chosen** profession and to recognise that it is indeed your **choice** – and to minimise the damage to you and those around you when life sometimes, inevitably, goes wrong.

Summarising ACT

We're reaching the end of our whistle-stop tour of ACT. Hopefully, using the tools provided here, you've started to see a new way of considering your position in the world and recognise that you *can* build the psychological flexibility and resilience needed to thrive in the challenging world of medicine – or to change direction entirely. To conclude we'll explore two final but vital points; the definition and function of psychological flexibility and the concept of a choice point.

Psychological flexibility

Life is thrust upon each one of us without ceremony from the moment of conception. We are born into the world, and throughout our short time on this planet we fill our lives with many things. Whatever we hold onto as our core values, and however we chose to spend our time on Earth, there are certain inevitabilities that all of us must face.

The first is death; we are undeniably and irrevocably going to die one day. Our time is mercilessly brief. We get only eighty or so years to appreciate the autumn leaves and the summer sun before our bodies fail and re-join the earth. While we may not consciously experience our own death, we will inevitably experience others. Loved ones, close friends and patients will pass away before us, sometimes even under our care.

The second is pain; our bodies are beautifully adapted to sense and empathise with pain. At the most basic level consider physical pain – even if we are fortunate and don't suffer any major accidents or painful diseases ourselves, we *will* still face the pain our patients suffer. Beyond this, we will *also* experience psychological pain or distress in our own lives for a myriad of reasons, from bereavement to stress to burnout.

Every life will inevitably encounter challenge and hardship in some capacity. The entire point of ACT is to promote psychological flexibility so that *when* these challenging events occur, we accept them openly, face them without fusing with them, and continue to work despite them towards a rich, full and meaningful life.

Choice point

The concept of the choice point is adapted from Dr Russ Harris and represents how to use all the skills learnt in ACT during a moment of crisis or distress. It utilises the core processes of the Hexaflex to consider how the way we react to an event or stimulus can help us work towards our values – or disrupt and move away from them.

The choice point starts with an event. This may be unwanted thoughts and feelings, or it may be a physical situation. From this point there are two potential routes; actions that move us **towards** our values and those that move us **away** from them.

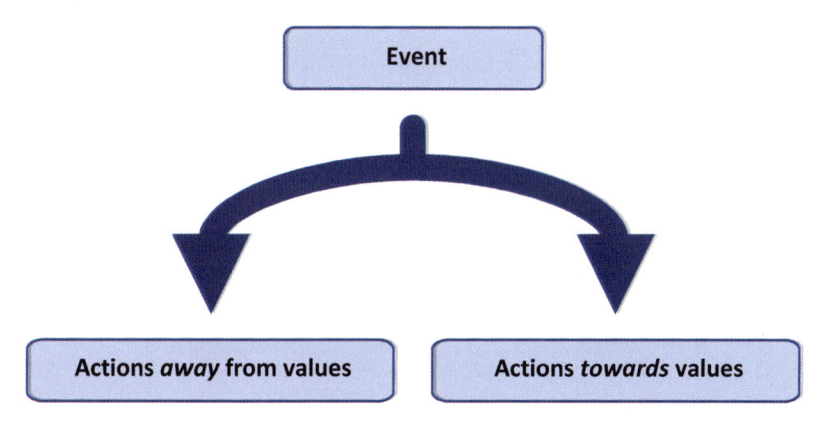

```
                    Event
                   /     \
                  ↓       ↓
   Actions away from values    Actions towards values
```

It sounds simple and, quite frankly, it is – however recognising and putting it into effect in the heat of the moment takes work and practice. The first key part of the choice point is recognising that *you* have a choice in the way you react to these scenarios. Let's illustrate with an example:

> **Starting point**
> A patient is rude/abusive towards you

It is so easy to feel disenfranchised or angry at the patient. It may even seem unjust (fairness or equality may well be one of your core values) that they get to treat you or other staff members this way, when you are trying your best to help them.

There are several ways you can approach this event:

- you could become angry yourself and shout
- you could refuse to treat the patient
- you could treat the patient begrudgingly and with resentment

THESE REACTIONS ARE NATURAL AND PART OF A NORMAL HUMAN RESPONSE

BUT they all have one thing in common; moving you **away** from your inherent value of care. If you momentarily indulged your fantasy of shouting back at your patient, for a few minutes you might feel vindicated and justified, but this won't last. You won't be a richer or better person for it.

The alternative offered by the choice point is acting **towards** your values and providing the patient with the same, high-quality care you offer every patient, but doing it *for yourself* – exercising your core value of care. You don't need to debate with or de-escalate the patient, but simply treating them calmly to the best of your abilities will engage you with your core values, and you will feel far more fulfilled and satisfied with the results. You get to be who you fundamentally are, whoever *they* are choosing to be.

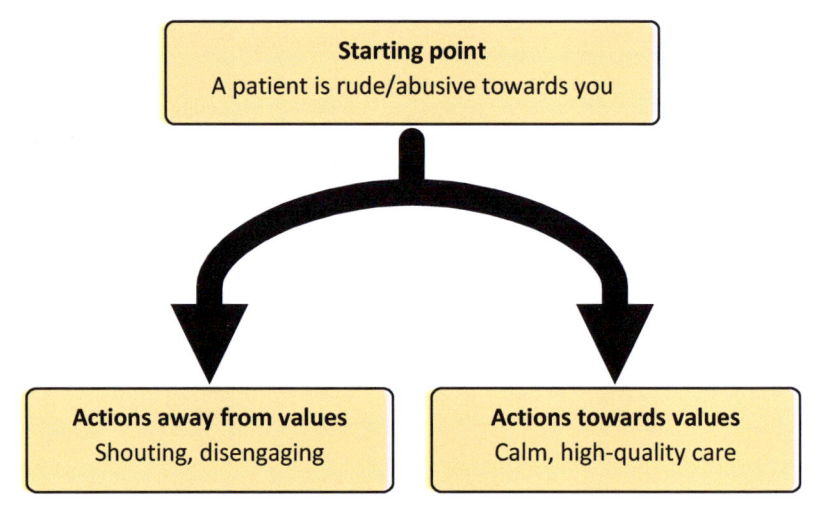

```
          ┌─────────────────────────────────────┐
          │          Starting point             │
          │ A patient is rude/abusive towards you│
          └─────────────────────────────────────┘
                   ↙              ↘
┌──────────────────────────┐  ┌──────────────────────────┐
│ Actions away from values │  │  Actions towards values  │
│  Shouting, disengaging   │  │   Calm, high-quality care│
└──────────────────────────┘  └──────────────────────────┘
```

It is very easy to describe this stream of events, but the choice point is not an infallible tool by which all our issues will be solved. There are many things to consider and sometimes the only action we can bring ourselves to take may be **away** from our values.

This is normal and expected.

Life is impossibly complex and presents us with challenges which demand instantaneous reactions. Practicing ACT can help improve your chances of reacting in a way that leads you towards your values. It can give you the tools to take those vital few seconds to stop and think, and react with a grounded and engaged mind – whilst recognising that there will be occasions when you act away from your values, because sometimes that is the only option that the universe leaves us! Don't feel beaten down by this – feel liberated that *you* have the choice to be what you want to be, and how everyone else wants to act is entirely up to them.

By slowly developing these processes you give yourself the best chance of catching your mind before it forces you away from who you are and want to be. Ultimately, being and living according to our fundamental values is the most important thing we can do to live a more rich, full and meaningful life. Taking the time to remind ourselves of what our values are, so we identify the choices which will make us more fulfilled and flexible human beings, is precious time well spent.

Lastly, let's take a look at some examples of how ACT may look in real time, at how a conflict can look different when we utilise all of the core processes. Of course, **ACT is not a flowchart**. These diagrams are meant to demonstrate one of a million ways that ACT can be used within a challenging situation. There simply isn't room in a book to show all the possible scenarios!

Acceptance and Commitment Skills for Medicine

Examples of ACT in action

This diagram illustrates each step with a core process of the ACT model to help you envisage how a conflict can be negotiated using ACT.

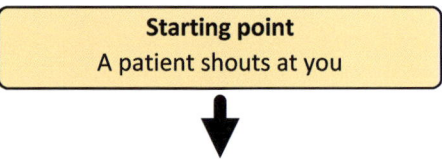

Starting point
A patient shouts at you

⬇

Contact with the present moment
Take a second to ground yourself and focus on *what is happening*

⬇

Acceptance
Allow yourself to experience the inevitable feelings of anger and dissatisfaction, but don't engage with them

⬇

Defusion
Distance yourself from those feelings and recognise them as just that, thoughts and feelings that don't reflect reality/aren't helpful

⬇

Values
Consider your core values, what action works towards the most fulfilling life for you?

⬇

Self-as-context
Observe yourself from an outsider's view

⬇

Committed ACTion
Engage with all the points above to act in a way that reflects and guides you towards your core values

⬇

End point
Action towards your values

Examples of ACT in action

Here's another diagram of an example of how you could use ACT.

Starting point
You are unsuccessful during a procedure

⬇

Contact with the present moment
Take a second to ground yourself and focus on *what is happening*

⬇

Defusion
Listen to your thoughts, but don't dwell on them – try using the 'thanking the brain' technique if there are intrusive or derogatory thoughts about yourself

⬇

Self-as-context
Observe yourself from a non-judgemental outsider's view, how would you feel if a colleague was in a similar scenario?

⬇

Acceptance
Recognise that you are not and cannot be perfect

⬇

Values
Consider your core values and how you can now act towards them – is this an opportunity for learning or self-improvement? The fact that you failed does not negate the fact that you tried and you care

⬇

Committed ACTion
Engage with all the points above to act in a way that reflects and guides you towards your core values

⬇

End point
Action towards your values

ACT IS <u>NOT</u> A FLOW CHART

Each of the core processes take place simultaneously and all act together to promote and improve psychological flexibility. Remember that ACT is not a step-by-step road to success, nor is it a formulaic guarantee of a constant calm mind. It is a psychological tool and way of viewing our world that requires patience and practice. It is highly researched, versatile and I hope helps bring you comfort, focus and stability in a world that can often be uncomfortable, distracting, and unstable.

And with that we've reached the end of our short handbook of ACT. Although this account is brief, I hope you have found it interesting and enlightening. Before you do anything else, take a second to put the book down and sit as upright as possible. Stretch out your back and take a deep breath to the bottom of your lungs. After this, pick up the book again.

Give yourself time to think. There is a great deal to take in. You may feel that some of the sections or exercises were more applicable to you than others were. I encourage you to engage with whatever chimed with you and felt the most productive. Take time to explore each exercise and gain more understanding about yourself. If you want to know more about ACT, there is a wealth of resources available to help you.

All change begins with the first step. Use your new knowledge of ACT to discover and explore what you truly value, and act towards it to give yourself a richer and more fulfilling experience of life. I wish you all the best of luck.

With thanks,

Dr James Fullick

In memorandum

Medicine is one of the most challenging fields to work in and has a high degree of dissatisfaction, burnout and stress associated with it. Whatever role you play within the healthcare environment, you are exposed to pain and suffering in levels no one should be expected to endure. We soak up long shifts, abusive patients, an unsympathetic media and constant exposure to people at the lowest points in their lives. The COVID-19 pandemic has only exacerbated the stress the healthcare system is under and highlighted how fragile and human we all are.

In some circumstances this distress reaches such intensity that it drives us to take the most extreme of actions. In England and Wales alone, in 2019 there were nearly 150 medical personnel who experienced grief and anguish so great that they actively ended their own lives. Looking at previous years this number is not unusual, and numbers for 2020 and beyond paint an even bleaker picture. Thinking back to Dunbar's number earlier in this book, our brains have evolved to form emotional connections with a *maximum* of 150 people. Each year enough medical staff commit suicide that it would entirely dominate our brains capacity to meet and know each of them. We are, from a neuropsychological point of view, unable to comprehend the number of medical staff who kill themselves each year.

There are around 950 hospitals within England and Wales, which means in an average career of 40 years you will see six staff suicides in the hospital you work. Look around you when you walk the corridors and take a moment to think. Be kind to yourself and to each of the people you meet – you never know who might be close to the brink. I hope that something in this book will help to ensure that you are never among them.

Where to find help

Help can mean many things, and different people need different levels of support at different times in their lives. This page signposts some of the resources available to help you navigate the challenges a life in medicine throws at you.

Remember – you are not alone and you are not beyond help.

If you feel you cannot go on and are in immediate danger of high-risk or suicidal behaviour, please call 999 or 111

National Suicide Prevention Helpline UK

www.spuk.org.uk
0800 689 5652 (phone lines open 24/7)

Samaritans

www.samaritans.org

BMA wellbeing

www.bma.org.uk/advice-and-support/your-wellbeing

BMA counselling and support line (24/7)

0330 123 1245

RCN Advice and Support

www.rcn.org.uk/Get-Help

Help within the NHS

Your line manager, educational or clinical supervisor will have training and contacts to help you. Telling people that you are struggling is *not* a sign of weakness and will enable them to provide you with the support you need.

Within your trust there will be a support network – you can either ask to be referred or refer yourself through a designated and confidential email. They are perfectly placed to offer support, therapy and guidance to help you when you need it most.

Further reading

The Happiness Trap by Dr Russ Harris

A more complete look at ACT by one of the most well-published researchers in the field. An excellent expansion on the points raised above aimed at the general public and exploring the flawed concept of 'happiness' and the modern obsession with the pursuit of it.

The Reality Slap by Dr Russ Harris

Another excellent book by Dr Harris, focussing more on the use of ACT following significant or traumatic life events. An excellent exploration of how to use ACT while facing adversity, and the journey to recovery.

ACT Made Simple by Dr Russ Harris

A textbook for psychologists on the principles and concepts surrounding ACT and its history. It delivers a brilliantly written, more in-depth look at ACT for those who are interested in expanding their knowledge of ACT with a more academic approach.

Acceptance and Commitment Skills for Perfectionism and High-achieving Behaviours by Dr Patricia Ona

An interesting read for those of us who find that typical 'type A' personality traits can obscure or confound our enjoyment of life. Not written to dissuade or demonise the driven or the dedicated, but instead full of useful tips and considerations of how to manage others and ourselves when our minds are full of such thoughts and feelings.

ACT in Context Podcast - Association for Contextual Behaviour Science

ACT in Context is a freely available podcast. Its episodes take listeners on a journey from the history and development of ACT through its clinical application and the future of the work. A wonderful guide and full of interesting speakers including Steven Hayes and Russ Harris.

ACTivate your life by Dr Joe Oliver, Dr Eric Morris and Jon Hill

A manual of ACT with a plethora of exercises and character stories of how you can use the core processes to frame and set your life in a direction that is truly meaningful to you.

References

A-tjak JG, Davis ML, Morina N, Powers MB, Smits JA, Emmelkamp PM. A meta-analysis of the efficacy of acceptance and commitment therapy for clinically relevant mental and physical health problems. Psychotherapy and psychosomatics. 2015;84(1):30-6.

Bai Z, Luo S, Zhang L, Wu S, Chi I. Acceptance and commitment therapy (ACT) to reduce depression: A systematic review and meta-analysis. Journal of Affective Disorders. 2020;260:728-37.

Blackledge JT. An introduction to relational frame theory: Basics and applications. The Behavior Analyst Today. 2003;3(4):421.

Dunbar RI. Neocortex size as a constraint on group size in primates. Journal of human evolution. 1992 Jun 1;22(6):469-93.

Hain D, Gallego-Flores T, Klinkmann M, Macias A, Ciirdaeva E, Arends A, Thum C, Tushev G, Kretschmer F, Tosches MA, Laurent G. Molecular diversity and evolution of neuron types in the amniote brain. Science. 2022 Sep 2;377(6610):8202.

Harris R. ACT Made Simple. Oakland CA: New Harbinger. 2009

Hayes SC, Berens NM. Why relational frame theory alters the relationship between basic and applied behavioral psychology. International Journal of Psychology and Psychological Therapy. 2004;4(2):341-53.

Howell AJ, Passmore HA. Acceptance and commitment training (ACT) as a positive psychological intervention: A systematic review and initial meta-analysis regarding ACT's role in well-being promotion among university students. Journal of Happiness Studies. 2019 Aug;20(6):1995-2010.

Kentish-Barnes N, Chevret S, Valade S, Jaber S, Kerhuel L, Guisset O, Martin M, Mazaud A, Papazian L, Argaud L, Demoule A. A three-step support strategy for relatives of patients dying in the intensive care unit: a cluster randomised trial. The Lancet. 2022 Feb 12;399(10325):656-64.

Lindenfors P, Wartel A, Lind J. 'Dunbar's number' deconstructed. Biology Letters. 2021 May 5;17(5):20210158.

Maslow AH. A Theory of Human Motivation. Psychological Review. 1943;50, 370-396.

Price D, Wagstaff CR, Thelwell RC. "What if I Get Injured?": An Acceptance and Commitment Therapy Approach for Fear of Injury With a Semi-Elite Youth Snowboarder. Case Studies in Sport and Exercise Psychology. 2022 Jan 1;6(1):12-20.

Further reading and references

Photo credits

With sincere thanks to Mike Hawley for his beautiful picture of a wolf in the 'trapped' exercise and to Tony, my father, for most of the other stunning photos in this book.

Thanks also to Pixabay artists:
OpenClipart-Vectors
Clker-Free-Vector-Images
GDJ
guvo59
TiagoCipriano
mohammed_hassan
gdakaska
TravelCoffeeBook

for photographs and vector-based graphics used in diagrams and illustrations.

Acknowledgements

I first started writing this book as a very personal part of my recovery from burnout. It was never meant to be anything more than some notes on reading about ACT and a few scribbles on my thoughts and feelings. It began to develop into more when I recognised how much ACT had actually helped me in my day-to-day life. I felt it was too important to keep to myself. It seems ridiculous in many ways that a doctor should be writing on psychotherapy, especially one who was receiving therapy himself. Several people convinced me otherwise and encouraged me to keep writing. I am eternally grateful to all of them for their help in making this book a reality and in their support during an incredibly trying part of my life.

My first thanks are to my wonderful wife, Sarah, who has offered continual love and support despite all of the trials that medicine has thrown at us. Her incredible efforts have kept our family sane and safe, and I could not have managed this without her. The tenacity and drive she shows is a constant inspiration to me.

I owe tremendous thanks to my mother, Ann, who, as an internationally published author herself, provided me with reams of helpful advice and editing, along with encouraging me to pursue this project to the end. Her wisdom and patience are bottomless and without her this book would not have happened. The same gratitude goes to my father, Tony, who provided me with gentle guidance on the formatting and publishing details, along with supplying most of the wonderful pictures within the book.

Dr Claire Delduca has been kindness and compassion itself with my rather clumsy handling of her profession. She has been instrumental in giving me the confidence to move this book forward, and in empowering me to realise that taking a rope that is thrown to you is not a sign of weakness.

My sincere thanks to those who took time out of their schedules to read and offer their expert opinions on this work. Dr Jack Parry-Jones has consistently offered his support as a senior clinician and his enthusiasm for this book have helped me to push forward in times when it felt impossible. Professor Marcus Grace is a deeply respected colleague who provided me with an excellent background on educational theory and generous amounts of encouragement. I sincerely thank him for taking time out of his research schedule to read through and offer pertinent advice for this work. I would like to offer special thanks to Dr Joe Oliver, who as one of the leading figures in ACT and a distinguished consultant psychologist took the time to read and provide such glowing feedback. His belief in this project and his expert opinion have been vital to the publication of this book. I am eternally grateful to all those who have supported me with their expertise and guidance through this endeavour. I stand on the shoulders of giants.

To all my colleagues and friends who have been there for me during these tough times, and to friends and family who have been lost – thank you all for your influence, advice and compassion.

And finally, to my darling daughter – for filling my heart with love and making me realise just how important it is to look for the sunshine.

Appendix

Acceptance To be open and accepting of myself and others	**Assertiveness** To respectfully stand up for my rights	**Authenticity** To be genuine and true to myself	**Beauty** To nurture/create beauty in myself/others
Caring To be considerate and kind to myself/others	**Challenge** To compete to grow, learn and improve	**Compassion** To act with kindness to those who are suffering	**Conformity** To be respectful and obedient to rules/obligations
Cooperation To collaborate and work together with others	**Creativity** To innovate and make or think of things differently	**Curiosity** To be open-minded and want to explore and discover	**Encouragement** To encourage and reward behaviour I value
Equality To treat myself as equal to others and vice versa	**Excitement** To seek/create exciting experiences	**Fairness** To be fair to myself and others	**Fitness** To improve my physical health and wellbeing
Freedom To live freely and be able to choose how I behave	**Friendliness** To be compassionate and agreeable to others	**Fun** To seek/create enjoyable activities	**Humour** To see and engage in the humorous side to life
Humility To be modest or humble	**Industry** To be hard working and dedicated	**Intimacy** To share myself emotionally with those close to me	**Love** To show affection to myself and those I care about
Order To be orderly and organised	**Patience** To wait calmly for what I want	**Pleasure** To create enjoyable things for myself and others	**Respect** To be considerate to others and expect the same back
Responsibility To be accountable for my actions	**Safety** To protect others and avoid accidents	**Sexuality** To express or explore my sexual drive/libido	**Spirituality** To explore or connect with a religion or higher power

Appendix

Not Important	Some Importance	Very important

Top 5 values	Most important value

Notes

Notes

Printed in Great Britain
by Amazon